Faithfulness

by
Dr. Ed Dufresne

Ed Dufresne Ministries
Temecula, California

Unless otherwise indicated,
all Scripture quotations are taken from
the *King James Version* of the Bible.

Copyright © 1981 by Ed Dufresne Ministries
P.O. Box 186
Temecula, California 92593

Second Edition
Second Printing--1994

ISBN 0-89274-212-7

Published by Ed Dufresne Ministries
P. O. Box 186
Temecula, California 92593

Please write to obtain an order form to request other publications.

Printed in the United States
All Rights Reserved

Contents

Foreword   7

1 Faithfulness   11

2 Integrity   25

3 Obedience or Rebellion?   39

Foreword

One of the greatest needs in the Church today is faithful workers. Pastors face discouragement as a constant enemy because people have not been obedient and faithful in the ministry of helps.

The Word of God promises blessings and promotion for those that will be faithful. This book speaks to the heart of everyone who would want to be successful in the ministry of the Lord Jesus Christ.

The Publisher

*I would like to dedicate this book to
my wife Nancy Dufresne who has the
real spirit of FAITHFULNESS.
Thank you Nancy for being a faithful wife.*

Faithfulness

1
Faithfulness

Wherefore he saith, When he ascended up on high, he led captivity captive, and gave gifts unto men.

[Now that he ascended, what is it but that he also descended first into the lower parts of the earth?

He that descended is the same also that ascended up far above all heavens, that he might fill all things.]
Ephesians 4:8-10

Notice verse 8 says that the Lord gave *gifts* unto men. What are these gifts? Verses 11 and 12 tell us:

Faithfulness

He gave some, apostles; and some, prophets; and some, evangelists; and some, pastors and teachers;
For the perfecting of the saints, for the work of the ministry, for the edifying of the body of Christ.

Every minister of the Gospel is a gift to the Church. When God first began to deal with me about preaching the Gospel, I had such a bad image of myself that I certainly couldn't see myself as a gift to the Church.

I had to renew my mind to the Word of God and build into my spirit the reality that I was anointed of God to preach the Gospel of Jesus Christ.

Before you can have any success as a pastor or teacher, you must know in your own heart that you are a gift to the Body of Christ. If you don't believe it now, then keep building that truth into your spirit until all the doubt is driven out.

Just as the anointing of Elijah was transferred to Elisha, so was the fivefold mantle of ministry — apostle, prophet, evangelist, pastor, and

Faithfulness

teacher — dropped upon men when Jesus ascended to heaven.

If you are in one of the classes listed here in Ephesians 4:11, then that mantle was dropped on you. You are one of those gifts, and you are responsible for that gift to the Body of Christ.

Many people today are not faithful to their calling.

According to the glorious gospel of the blessed God, which was committed to my trust.

And I thank Christ Jesus our Lord, who hath enabled me, for that he counted me faithful, putting me into the ministry.

1 Timothy 1:11,12

It's important to be faithful, no matter where you are or what you do.

When I first got saved, I loved the Lord so much that I wanted to do anything I could for Him, so He put me in charge of cleaning the toilets in my

Faithfulness

church. [Never ask to do something unless you intend to follow through!]

For over a year I was faithful in cleaning the toilets in that church. I thanked God that He counted me worthy to serve Him; and for being faithful in it, the Lord told me that He was going to bless whatever I set my hand to. And He did!

I got so blessed that I ended up with two trucks and 15 employees in my new toilet business! As the Apostle Paul wrote to Timothy, I thank Christ Jesus, my Lord, Who has enabled me to clean the toilets, for He counted me *faithful*, putting me into the ministry.

I was also in charge of cleaning the carpets and shining the pulpit. One night while working, I was thanking the Lord for my pastor, and God told me He had counted me faithful and was going to promote me to door greeter. So I was faithful as a door greeter!

You know, it makes an impression on people how they are met at the door. Even when people wouldn't offer their hand, I would

Faithfulness

just grab them and hug them and tell them I loved them.

When the Lord found me faithful as a door greeter, He promoted me to deacon. Then He said, "Son, I've counted you faithful in these three things. Now you are going to preach the Gospel."

No matter what you are called to do — whether it's toilet detail, deacon, pastor, or floor sweeper — be faithful in it. One of the biggest problems in many churches is that the pastor doesn't have faithful workers.

The ministry of helps is just as important to God as the ministry of pastor. Praise God for the men who have been faithful in holding another man's coat!

In Exodus 17:8-13, Israel fought against Amalek. Because Moses couldn't get the job done alone, God provided faithful men to hold up his arms until the sun went down — and Israel prevailed over the enemy.

Faithfulness

When a church has a group of faithful workers, it can prevail over an entire town. The Lord did a pruning on my ministry and it seemed like half the church was going to leave; but when the purging was over, I was left with a faithful group of people.

So the last shall be first, and first last: for many be called, but few chosen.
Matthew 20:16

God does not want you to push your ministry. Promote the Word and you will be promoted. But on the other hand, I am convinced that few are chosen because many who are called have a lack of faithfulness.

I would consider it a great honor for God to tell me to be faithful to a man of God and give him all the help he needs. One of the biggest enemies a pastor faces is discouragement. That's why God puts men into the ministry of helps and expects them to be faithful in upholding the pastor.

Proverbs 28:20 says, *A faithful man shall abound with blessings.*

Faithfulness

Years ago I was faithful when God told me to go from California to Oregon and preach to twelve people. For one year I pastored a group of people in Smith Valley, out where there was nothing but ranches.

We met in homes. The Indians would come down from the hills, and I would pastor those people every Sunday night. I was faithful to them.

There were times when I would say, "Lord, am I gonna be stuck with these people way out here in the boonies?"

It's so easy to start looking at the numbers. I had a problem with that. We say, "I don't have 20,000 people in my church, so I guess I'm not successful." If you get one person saved every Sunday, you're having success!

While I was preaching back then, it was so easy to get my eyes on other men's ministries. I was always watching other people to see how they would do things in their ministries; then I would try to imitate them, thinking it would

Faithfulness

bring me the same success. Finally, God told me that if I kept doing that, it would destroy my ministry. I had to be faithful to what God told *me* to do. So I learned to relax and be faithful where I was.

You need to let God develop your personality and your ministry. If you keep your eyes on men, they'll fail you. But God knows how to do it. Remember, it will take some time for God to build character in you. Be faithful with the little things and watch God load it on you.

He that is faithful in that which is least is faithful also in much: and he that is unjust in the least is unjust also in much.

If therefore ye have not been faithful in the unrighteous mammon, who will commit to your trust the true riches?

And if ye have not been faithful in that which is another man's who shall give you that which is your own?

Luke 16:10-12

Faithfulness

Some men are driven with ambition to get to the top. The ministries should be at the top in the end result, but many people are just driven to out do other people. We should want to help other ministers and rejoice with them when they get blessed. We have to get rid of this competitive attitude and just be faithful in doing what God has told us to do.

His lord said unto him, Well done, thou good and faithful servant: thou hast been faithful over a few things, I will make thee ruler over many things: enter thou into the joy of thy lord.

Matthew 25:21

This is what the Lord meant when He said those who are last shall be first. Though you are only in charge of the little things at the end of the line, God will exalt you much quicker than any man could.

If God counts you faithful in what He told you to do, I can guarantee you that He will promote you. You may feel inadequate for your position; but if God put you there, then you can fulfill it. He will give you the tools and He will give you the speech.

Faithfulness

After I experienced how it feels to be humiliated before people, I told God I would never preach again.

But the Lord said, "You must be more worried about what they think of you than what they think of My Word. Now get out there and put it out!"

So I did, and He has given me the tools and the speech to do it with.

God has counted me faithful, just as He will count you faithful. All you have to do is make the quality decision to be faithful where He puts you and let Him promote you.

Nothing could be more rewarding than to hear Jesus say to you, "Well done, thou good and faithful servant."

*And as for me,
thou upholdest me in mine
integrity,
and settest me before thy face
for ever.*

Psalm 41:12

2
Integrity

For the word of God is quick, and powerful, sharper than any two-edged sword, piercing even to the dividing asunder of soul and spirit, and of the joints and marrow, and is a discerner of the thoughts and intents of the heart.

Hebrews 4:12

God's Word is powerful, and there is integrity behind it. It's something you can count on. You might just as well establish in your heart the fact that God never changes, because

Faithfulness

He doesn't — and neither does His Word! God meant what He said and said what He meant.

All of us have had temptations in our lives to be "down in the dumps" and have "the blues." We don't have to be, but most of us have been at some point in our lives. But as soon as we begin to confess the Word of God, the powerful force of faith rises up in our spirits and drives out that discouragement. That happens because God is a man of His Word. What He said He would do, He *will* do!

But what about the integrity of your word? Jeremiah 1:12 says, *Then said the Lord unto me, Thou hast well seen: for I will hasten my word to perform it.* This verse in The Amplified Bible says, *"For I am alert and active, watching over My word to perform it."*

One day the Lord said to me, "I hasten My Word to perform it. Now, how about you? Do you hasten to keep your own word?"

Well, God nailed me in that area! Here I am, pastoring a church, traveling all over the country

Integrity

to preach the Word of God, and all of a sudden God calls me a liar!

I said, "What are You talking about, God?"

Then He reminded me of how I had promised to do something for someone but never did. To God, that's lying. Since that day, I have been a stickler about keeping my word.

Numbers 23:19 says, *God is not a man, that he should lie.* If we are to be imitators of Him, as stated in Ephesians 5:1, then we ought to keep our word, too! God told me that if we never keep our own word, we will never be able to believe His Word.

You will never grow spiritually until you watch over the words that come out your mouth. If you are being sloppy about your word, how can you ever take God's Word seriously?

As I travel across the country, people come to me all the time promising to do this or that for the ministry; yet they never keep their word. Some people I have come to know over the years are so wishy-washy with their words that I can't trust them.

If I tell someone I'm going to buy them something, I'll do it if it harelips the devil! Even if it meant getting a second job and working with my hands to get the money, I would do it to keep my word.

When you tell someone you're going to do something, but then don't do it, you break down your own faith. You won't be able to trust in God's Word because you can't trust your own.

There are other people I know whose word is good. If they told me to wait for them on the roof of the church building at noon tomorrow so they could give me a gift, I would be there waiting!

What happened to the day when a handshake between two men was all they needed to assure them that their deal would

Integrity

come to pass? Their integrity was on the line, and they knew it! Back then, their integrity meant something to them.

Psalm 119:89 says, *For ever, O Lord, thy word is settled in heaven.*

Is your word settled?

When you look at a successful man, you will find that he is healthy and prosperous, that he has a happy home, and most of all that he has integrity about him. That's how he got to be successful in the first place. His word is settled.

Psalm 141:3 says, *Set a watch, O Lord, before my mouth; keep the door of my lips.* We need to learn to guard our words and listen to what we are saying.

Right here, let me make one thing clear: Don't do something just because I did — do it because you believe what God has said in His Word. Many people try to imitate other people's experiences, they act on what another person did instead of acting on God's Word. You know what level you are on spiritually. God might tell you to have an operation. You have to act according to your faith.

Death and life are in the power of the tongue: and they that love it shall eat the fruit thereof.
Proverbs 18:21

Are you prepared to eat the fruit of your mouth?

Proverbs 19:9 says, *A false witness shall not be unpunished, and he that speaketh lies shall perish.* God will always love you; it's the lying that He hates. If you've taken time to entertain the devil's lies, then just repent and go on.

God wants us to start building character into ourselves so that we have integrity. It's about time that the Church realizes the integrity of God's Word; but it won't happen until we learn to say No! to the devil and his lies and start walking according to God's will. When we do, people will be coming to us seeking to have what we have.

Integrity

David said, "Lord, put a guard over my mouth!" If you have to, hire a security guard to watch over everything that comes out your mouth! My wife is my guard. As soon as unbelief comes out of my mouth, she is right there to tell me to swallow it!

If this sounds extreme to you, then I guess Jesus was an extremist. He watched over every word that came out of His mouth.

In John's Gospel, chapter 11, when Jesus learned that His good friend Lazarus was sick, He never got in a hurry. He didn't start spouting statements of unbelief. He simply said, *This sickness is not unto death [v.4].*

Throughout the entire chapter, Jesus was surrounded by people who said one thing and believed another. His own disciples had no more faith in His words than Martha did. All of them proclaimed that He was the Son of God, yet no one believed the integrity of His Word.

Many people, including the disbelieving

Faithfulness

Jews, thought Jesus was weeping over the death of His friend, when actually He was grieved with their unbelief.

Through it all, Jesus never changed His word. Four days before, He had said that this sickness was not unto death. Then He called into the tomb with faith-filled words, bringing Lazarus back to life, He proved to those people that He was a man of His Word — and so was His Father!

How did all this come about? First of all, Jesus guarded His words. He said that which He desired to come to pass. Jesus also knew that God was a man of His Word and that He watches over His Word to perform it. Therefore, Jesus could trust His integrity and know from the start that whatever He said would come to pass.

If you start watching over your words and begin keeping your word to people, then you will know in your heart that you can believe in God's Word. Until you make the quality decision to be a man or woman of your word, you will be a miserable Christian.

Integrity

If you have made an appointment, with a person, but know you will be late, call and tell him.

Don't promise to give money out of emotion. Give at the level of faith where you are, so you won't get under condemnation if you can't keep your word.

When you agree to do something, make every effort to see it come to pass. God has put His integrity on the line. Now how about you?

Faithfulness

Confession

Father in heaven, I make the quality decision with Your help and by the help of Your Holy Spirit that I will be a man/woman of my word.

You said in Your Word, Father, that You hasten Your word to perform it. You also said that I am to be an imitator of You. Therefore, Lord, I will continually watch over my words to perform them and be a man/woman of integrity.

No idle promises will pass through my lips; but by the power of Your Word and the wisdom of Your Holy Spirit, I will say what I mean and mean what I say.

In the name of Jesus, I will be a man/woman of my word!

*If ye be willing and obedient,
ye shall eat the good of the land.*
                            Isaiah 1:19

3
Obedience or Rebellion?

The other morning as I was sitting in our church, getting ready to preach, the Holy Ghost suddenly rose up within me and said, "There's rebellion in the Body of Christ, and it stinks in the nostrils of God!"

And he took the book of the covenant, and read in the audience of the people: and they said, All that the Lord hath said will we do, and be obedient.

Exodus 24:7

Obedience will always create an atmosphere for miracles. There are always rewards that come along with obedience.

Faithfulness

People may think their pastor is crazy for laying people on the floor and running across their back, but they still see miracles! Why? Because he was obedient to what God said to do. If you try to do that without direction from the Holy Spirit, you will probably be sorry!

Once as I was praying for people in the prayer line, when I got to one woman, it was like somebody grabbed my hand and slapped her across the face! Her husband, who was standing next to her, was quite a bit larger than me, and my head was screaming, "My God, what did I do!" But because I was obedient to the Holy Spirit, the woman's jaw was completely healed. Obedience to the voice of God and His Word pays off.

For that they hated knowledge, and did not choose the fear of the Lord:

They would none of my counsel: they despised all my reproof.

Therefore shall they eat of the fruit of their own way, and be filled with their own devices.
Proverbs 1:29-31

Obedience or Rebellion?

Have you ever eaten the fruit of your own way instead of God's? I have done that and the Lord began to deal with me on it. He told me I needed to be obedient to my calling, not somebody else's. I would want to set up my own meetings without the Lord telling me to, just because another brother had done it down the road.

There is a price to pay for doing things your own way, instead of God's, and my price was having to pay for that meeting. Only eight people showed up — and half of them were my family! So I had to pick up the tab.

The Lord has really been showing me how there are preachers starting churches and training centers that God never told them to start. They are doing it just because it is popular. But God said that because of it, they will have to eat the fruit of their own way; and many have suffered by losing their ministries.

What we are talking about is an attitude of rebellion.

Faithfulness

One time I was in a car with someone who had installed a device to signal when a policeman with radar was ahead. As I was sitting there, minding my own business, the Holy Ghost rose up in me and said, "Those devices are rebellious."

I said, "What?"

He said, "When you're using them to break the speed limit, they're rebellious."

If you don't like to drive the speed limit, then I suggest that you start interceding and get the laws changed.

There is a spirit of rebellion in the world, and I'm sorry to say that it's even getting on the Christians.

One day when I was getting ready to speak at Jerry Savelle's church in Fort Worth, Texas, they handed me a little guest badge to wear so they could identify me.

I thought to myself, "Well, bless God, that's kind of childish, having to wear a little badge.

Obedience or Rebellion?

I'm not gonna wear that stupid thing." So I put it in my pocket.

That night after the meeting, I was lying in bed and couldn't go to sleep. The Lord said, "Rebellion, rebellion, rebellion. They ask you to do a simple thing like wear a badge to identify you, and you rebel. Why do you have to be so rebellious?"

When you let that spirit of rebellion get on you, it will guide your life. For instance, in special meetings an usher might have to come up to you and ask you to sit in a different section. How many times have you seen people get upset over a little thing like that? It's just a spirit of rebellion. God said He won't use us for big things if He can't trust us to be obedient with little things.

It is so important that we be obedient to what God tells each of us to do. When you get out of the will of God, you get out from under His protection. I want to live long on this earth.

There is an attitude of rebellion in the Church, and we have to see about changing that attitude.

Faithfulness

If ye be willing and obedient, ye shall eat the good of the land:

But if ye refuse and rebel, ye shall be devoured with the sword: for the mouth of the Lord hath spoken it.

Isaiah 1:19,20

The Lord gives us *two conditions for blessing:* We must be *willing* and we must be *obedient*.

But there are also *two conditions for cursing:* If you *refuse* and *rebel*, you shall be devoured.

A perfect example of a person who is willing and obedient and eating the good of the land is Jerry Savelle.

Jerry and his wife and children moved to Fort Worth in an old beat-up car to work for Kenneth Copeland. Nobody ever saw him working all night long. He would start by taking Brother Copeland to meetings and making sure everything was set up. [He was the only helper to do the running around.]

Obedience or Rebellion?

When the meeting was over, Jerry would put Brother Copeland in the car, rush him to the hotel; then he would come back, pick up all the tapes, load the sound equipment, put it in the truck, go back to his room and work all night long with a reel-to-reel tape recorder, getting those tape orders ready to send out. Early the next morning, he would pick up the prophet of God and get him ready for their next meeting.

Jerry was faithful. He did that week in and week out, month in and month out. He was obedient to what God told him to do. Today, Jerry has a ministry of his own that is growing steadily as he continues to obey the Word of God. You see, there are *always* rewards that come along with obedience.

On the other side of the coin, there is a man that I love with all my heart; but instead of fulfilling his ministry as God wanted him to do, he put his eyes on man and got into rebellion. Today, his ministry is null.

If he had been obedient to hold another man's coat, he would be on the scene today in

Faithfulness

his own ministry. Instead, he has been shoved off somewhere in a corner. Once in a while, he will come out to teach a Sunday School class.

In Ephesians, chapter 6, God is talking to the Church. If we will obey His Word, we will continually see the rewards that come with it. In verses 1-3 He says:

Children, obey your parents in the Lord: for this is right.

Honour thy father and mother; which is the first commandment with promise;

That it may be well with thee, and thou mayest live long on the earth.

I was raised in a home where both parents were alcoholics. My mother was in and out of mental institutions. As a child growing up, I learned to hate my mother. As the oldest, I had to do the dishes and change my brother's and sister's diapers. When I became a teenager, I wanted to go out and do things, but I had to stay home and take care of the kids.

Obedience or Rebellion?

If I had known then what I know now, I would have taken authority over the devil and cast him out of my mother's life, in the name of Jesus. But all I knew then was that I hated and resented her.

When I was born again, the Lord began to deal with me in this area. One day God showed me this third verse of Ephesians, chapter 6: *That it may be well with thee, and thou mayest live long on the earth.*

The Lord said, "Do you want to live long?"

I said, "Yes, Sir."

"Then be obedient to My Word. Honor your mother and father."

So I was obedient to what the Word says, and praise God for it! I went to my mother and told her I was sorry for the hatred that had been in my heart, that I was sorry for being so disrespectful and for treating her so bad. Then I said, "Mama, I'm a new creature in Christ now and I ask you to forgive me."

Faithfulness

It pays to be obedient to God's Word. My mother died not long after that, but she made Jesus Christ the Lord of her life two hours before she died. She has forgiven me, and now I intend to live long on this earth for being obedient to the Word.

The Lord has had me to preach this subject quite a bit recently as I travel across the nation. At a Full Gospel Businessmen's Advance I preached it to approximately 1400 men; and when I was through, about 500 crying men ran to the phones and called their mothers to get things straightened out.

You have to either obey the Word of God or pay the price.

Ephesians 6:4 says, *And, ye fathers, provoke not your children to wrath: but bring them up in the nurture and admonition of the Lord.*

Dake's Annotated Reference Bible says, "Provoke not your children to wrath. Avoid severity, anger, harshness, cruelty. Cruel parents generally have bad children."

Obedience or Rebellion?

Do you want to know why our jails are filled up? Because some kids got knocked around, beat up, and slammed in the head by their parents.

"Well, Brother Ed, that wouldn't happen in a Christian home."

Don't fool yourself! As a pastor, I counsel people who beat their children.

I'm observing people and learning all the time. What I see is Sister Bucketmouth who gets up in church and prophesies, giving a beautiful word from the Lord. Then I see that same sister outside with her children, who have been in Sunday School for three hours and have gotten a little cranky. I see her dragging them across the parking lot, yelling at them to shut up, jerking them around, slapping them in the head, and throwing them in the car.

That may sound funny, but it won't be so funny if those children end up in jail for being treated just that way.

Faithfulness

The Bible says to bring up your child in the *nurture* and admonition of the Lord. Nurture means "child-training, education, correcting." I'm not telling you to avoid spanking them. The Bible says to do it, but it doesn't say to do it cruelly. We just have to be obedient to what the Word says.

For many years, there was rebellion in our home between my oldest daughter and her mother and me, and there was good reason for it. Before my wife and I were saved, our little girl saw some terrible things happen in her home. She saw her mommy and daddy throwing things at each other — everything from knives to furniture!

After I got saved, I began to pray about how to bring my daughter back to me. The Lord said to just bring them up in the Word of God, to love them, put the Word around them, and use the rod of correction when they needed it. So I was obedient to the Word of God.

One night as I was preaching in our church, my daughter was sitting on the front row.

Obedience or Rebellion?

Towards the end of the meeting she started crying and weeping. The Holy Spirit came upon her and showed her that I was a minister of the Gospel and a man she could respect.

After the meeting, I went into the back room and Carole came running through the doors, jumped in my lap, threw her arms around me, and cried, "Daddy, Daddy, I love you, I love you!" She had never done that before. It came from our being obedient to the Word of God.

Oh, the rewards for being obedient! God said that if you bring up your children in the ways of the Lord, they will not depart from it.

I make it a point to pray for my children and confess the Word over them. My girls are not going to end up as prostitutes or on drugs. They are going to serve God. I have been obedient to do what the Word says and to preach it to others. The rewards are that my children are serving God.

Faithfulness

Ephesians 6:5-8 says:

Servants, be obedient to them that are your masters according to the flesh, with fear and trembling, in singleness of your heart, as unto Christ;

Not with eye service, as menpleasers; but as the servants of Christ, doing the will of God from the heart;

With good will doing service, as to the Lord, and not to men:

Knowing that whatsoever good thing any man doeth, the same shall he receive of the Lord, whether he be bond or free.

Notice that there are four scriptures speaking to the employee, but just one which speaks to the employer. I think the Holy Spirit is trying to get something across to the Church. There is an attitude in people — and I'm sorry to say, even with Christians — that the world owes them a living. If everyone would go to work Monday morning and put in eight good hours of work that we are being paid to do, we could stop inflation.

Obedience or Rebellion?

If you go into work with the attitude of working unto the Lord, you can change things on the job, no matter how bad they may seem. Maybe the reason your foreman is so ornery is because you haven't been interceding for him. You can put the Word of God on people and change things by interceding.

Ephesians 6:8 says, *Knowing that whatsoever good thing any man doeth, the same shall he receive of the Lord, whether he be bond or free.* If you are obedient to God's Word and treat your employer as if he were Jesus, you may end up owning the company! God will bless you for your obedience.

You need to uphold your employer just like you need to uphold your pastor. If you are in rebellion just because they ask you to wear a badge or sit in a certain section, then you need to cast out that spirit of rebellion. And you can't be rebellious toward your pastor either. He is a gift from God — the head of your church, the under-shepherd. It stinks in the nostrils of God when the people get into rebellion and won't support their pastor.

Faithfulness

Verse 9 of Ephesians 6 says, *And ye masters, do the same things unto them, forbearing threatening: knowing that your Master also is in heaven; neither is there respect of persons with him.* As an employer, if you treat your employees like they were Jesus, you will never have any problem with strife or rebellion.

Everybody wants to live in the flood of God's blessings; but the flood won't come unless you obey God and live by His Word. Just think about Ananias' obedience when the Spirit of God told him to go to Damascus and pray for Saul of Tarsus. [Acts 9:10-18.]

Ananias replied, in so many words, "Lord, he's a murderer! He's a killer!"

But when God tells us to do something, we have to be obedient, no matter what our opinion may be on the matter. Even when Ananias knew in his heart that Saul was a murderer, he still went to Damascus and prayed for him. God was able to work miracles by giving Saul of Tarsus his sight and making him one of the greatest preachers of that time.

Obedience or Rebellion?

Obedience always creates an atmosphere for miracles.

What if God told you to minister to an ex-convict, a man previously known as a dangerous criminal? Then when you were obedient, that man turned out to be another Oral Roberts. Oh, the rewards for being obedient!

We ministers and pastors have got to be obedient to the Word of God. Don't hold back on what God tells you to preach, even if you think your whole church will leave you.

The Lord told me to drive rebellion out of my church by preaching on love, so I preached on love for three months. I thought my church was going to empty out, but God just filled it back up!

Be sensitive to the Holy Spirit. When God tells you to do something, do it! If He doesn't give you special instruction, don't do something just because it is the popular thing to do.

Faithfulness

Remember, if you are willing and obedient, you shall eat the good of the land! God will bless you to overflowing.

Obedience or Rebellion?

If you would like to receive
Ed Dufresne's quarterly publication,
Jesus the Healer Newsletter, free and
postpaid, write:

Ed Dufresne Ministries
P. O. Box 186
Temecula, CA 92593

*Feel free to include your prayer
requests and comments when you write.*

Available From Ed Dufresne Ministries
Books by Dr. Ed Dufresne

Fresh Oil From Heaven

Praying God's Word

The Prophet, Friend of God

Devil Don't Touch My Stuff

There's a Healer in the House

Tell the People

Faithfulness

Anointings & Mantles

For a complete list of
books and tapes,
write to:

ED DUFRESNE MINISTRIES
P. O. Box 186, Temecula, CA 92593
or call (909)694-8799